Presented by the Powerhouse Museum in association

with Christian Dior, Paris and

the Union Française des Arts du Costume, Paris

Christian Dior

the magic of fashion

POWERHOUSE PUBLISHING

PUBLICATION

Design: MaD House Design
Editing: Meryl Potter
Translations: Joanna Savill (Genty, Ferré, exhibition catalogue listing) and Diana Mitchell (Kamitsis)
Photography: Sue Stafford*
Production coordination: Julie Donaldson*
Copyright: Dallas Cox*
Word processing: Anne Slam*
Printing: Bloxham & Chambers

Published in conjunction with the exhibition *Christian Dior: the magic of fashion* at the Powerhouse Museum
27 July – 23 October 1994.

EXHIBITION

Project director: Jane de Teliga*
Curators: Louise Mitchell*; Marika Genty (Christian Dior); Lydia Kamitsis (UFAC); Glynis Jones*
Design: Susan Freeman*
Coordination: Susan McMunn*
Graphic design: Colin Rowan*
Conservation: Suzanne Chee*
Audiovisual: Kathleen Phillips*
Editing: Karin Vesk*

* Powerhouse Museum staff

ACKNOWLEDGMENTS

The Powerhouse Museum gratefully acknowledges the assistance of the following: Judy Barraclough; Mrs Marjorie Birch; Nicole Bunbury; June Dally-Watkins; Patricia Harewood; Beril Jents; Sandra King; Paule Paulus; Sheila Scotter; Wolfgang Sievers; Rosemary Spittle; Mrs Sam Wood. Thanks also to: Edwina Baillieu; Sam Griffin; Michael Shmith; Georgina Weir; Joan Wreford.

Colleagues and institutions in Australia: Australian Film and Sound Archive, Annie Vass; Australian National Gallery, Michael Desmond, Roger Leong and Gael Newton; Coles Myer Ltd archives, Stella Barber and Angela Henrickson; David Jones Ltd archives, Barbara Horton; National Gallery of Victoria, Isobel Crombie, Robyn Healy and Susan van Wyck; University of Queensland, Margaret Maynard.

CIP
Dior, Christian
Christian Dior: the magic of fashion.

Bibliography.
ISBN 1 86317 048 0

1. Dior, Christian — Exhibitions. 2. Fashion designers — France — History — 20th century — Exhibitions. 3. Fashion — France — Paris — History — 20th century — Exhibitions. 4. Fashion — Australia — History — 20th century — Exhibitions. 5. Costume design — France — History — 20th century — Exhibitions. I. Powerhouse Museum II. Title.

746.92092

First published 1994
by Powerhouse Publishing
PO Box K346,
Haymarket
2000 NSW Australia

Every effort has been made to contact the copyright owners of and provide correct acknowledgment for the photographs reproduced in this publication. All inquiries should be made to Powerhouse Publishing.

ontents

Forewords

by Terence Measham, director Powerhouse Museum   **4**

Bernard Arnault, president Christian Dior   **4**

Pierre Bergé, president UFAC   **5**

The House of Dior today   **6**
by Gianfranco Ferré

Christian Dior: the magic of fashion   **8**
introduction by Louise Mitchell

Couture and elegance: the House of Christian Dior   **13**
by Marika Genty

Christian Dior: a new era in haute couture   **26**
by Lydia Kamitsis

Christian Dior and postwar Australia   **38**
by Louise Mitchell

Chronology: the Dior years 1946–1994   **54**
compiled by Marika Genty

Catalogue of the exhibition   **58**

Further reading   **64**

Photo credits   **64**

forewords

the Powerhouse Museum is delighted to be presenting the exhibition *Christian Dior: the magic of fashion* in association with Christian Dior, Paris and the Union Française des Arts du Costume (UFAC).

Christian Dior is undoubtedly the most famous name in twentieth century fashion. The Powerhouse Museum, which holds one of Australia's foremost collections of costume, is proud to stage this major retrospective of Dior. This is the first time such a significant collection of Dior gowns has been displayed outside Paris.

Drawn from the collections of Christian Dior and UFAC, the exhibition traces the remarkable decade of design by Christian Dior from 1947 to 1957 and brings it to the present with a selection of gowns by the House of Dior's later designers, Yves Saint Laurent, Marc Bohan and Gianfranco Ferré. A special section developed by the Powerhouse Museum focuses on Dior in postwar Australia, in particular the Dior parades held at David Jones in Sydney in 1948 and 1957.

The Powerhouse Museum is grateful for the cooperation of Christian Dior, Paris and the assistance of Michel-Henri Carriol, delegate for Christian Dior in Australia, in enabling this important exhibition to come to Australia.

I would also like to acknowledge the collaboration of the curators of the exhibition: Louise Mitchell, from the Powerhouse Museum, who worked on the exhibition in association with Marika Genty from Christian Dior and Lydia Kamitsis from UFAC; and Jane de Teliga who initiated and directed the project for the Powerhouse Museum.

Our grateful thanks go to all those who have generously supported the Christian Dior exhibition, particularly the following sponsors:

Air France • Union des Assurances de Paris • Parfums Christian Dior • Nine Network Australia • David Jones Australia • Hotel Inter-Continental.

Terence Measham
Director, Powerhouse Museum, Sydney

Christian Dior — the magical name that for forty-seven years now has been synonymous the world over with the enchantment of French fashion, elegance and style.

Regardless of the intrinsically fleeting nature of this creative sphere and the endless cycle of seasonal collections, the House of Christian Dior has somehow withstood the cruelty of time: season after season, Dior has, almost paradoxically, built its own timelessness, eschewing the ephemeral and placing itself squarely in the realm of tradition.

Despite the untimely death of its founder, the House of Dior has grown and branched out beyond its original field, that of haute couture, to acquire the far more global dimension it enjoys today.

I am always moved when I re-read the visionary words taken from Monsieur Dior's personal correspondence: 'In troubled times like ours, we must uphold our tradition of luxury, the jewel of our culture.'

Bernard Arnault
President, Christian Dior

Christian Dior did not invent haute couture, but it was incontestably he who fixed its rules and set its bounds. Thanks to him, fashion became an art form in France and is now part of our national heritage. He invented licensing, and his name, famous throughout the world, has become synonymous with elegance and creativity. His reign was to last only ten years (1947–1957), but he made his mark in such a way that even today it has lost nothing of its magic.

In 1955 Dior discovered the talent of a young man as yet unheard of, Yves Saint Laurent. He took him on, made him his closest assistant and then his avowed successor. At the beginning of their collaboration, Yves Saint Laurent created a dress, photographed by Richard Avedon for *Harper's Bazaar* on 30 August 1955 in the now famous composition 'Dovima and the elephants'. It was therefore quite natural, when Dior died in 1957, that Yves Saint Laurent should succeed him.

The Union Française des Arts du Costume (UFAC), which came into being in 1948, a year after the Dior adventure began, set itself the task of perpetuating French creativity.

UFAC has been able to preserve thousands of pieces of clothing, providing us today with a broad view of creative fashion history. Our collections of clothes and documentary resources make up one of the world's biggest reference centres, which designers continue to add to, season after season. As its custodian, UFAC has made this heritage available for nearly fifty years by taking part in international events like *Christian Dior: the magic of fashion* at the Powerhouse Museum in Sydney.

I trust that this exhibition in Australia will give a broad public the opportunity to admire some of the most original and interesting works of art of our times, and to appreciate the emergence, two years after the end of the Second World War, of a designer whose name would resound like thunder down the decades.

Pierre Bergé
President, Yves Saint Laurent
President, the Union Française des Arts du Costume, Paris

the House of Dior today by Gianfranco Ferré*

The artists I admire are those who try to unleash a certain interplay in their work, creating within the parameters of tradition and innovation.

When I came to Dior my initial concern was to bring into contemporary focus what was generally considered to be a magical universe. By using trousers, for example, a fairly masculine garment, I was able to revive the classic Dior suit. Combined with a waisted jacket, highlighted by a blouse in organza or lace, they create the sort of shape I really like: something that is both romantic and contemporary, but remains extremely feminine.

Everything Christian Dior produced works on this basic polarity between strength and softness, tradition and innovation. He could put together a collection featuring a gown with the purest of lines alongside one sprinkled with mock daisies, in a *trompe l'oeil* effect. In the same vein, he would blend artificial forms with traditional materials and inject an air of modernity into every one of his designs.

That's my point of departure too. When designing my own collections I am constantly reworking the theme of contrasts.

There are many links between my work and that of Christian Dior. As a former architect I am accustomed to developing my designs in two steps, starting from research and experimentation and making free, flowing sketches. I concur with Christian Dior's words when he said: 'Sketches are the first form of an idea.'[1] They are the expression of a look, a line, a stance. They are a guide to volume and proportion. I create moving shapes and lines.

The next phase is pure technique, the architectural plan as it were, where the fabric of the design takes on volume and form.

The expertise of the Dior workrooms, heirs to the full tradition of couture, means the professional skills and techniques of the past can be applied to the present. Thanks to their skills, I can conjugate and decline lines, shapes and collections adapted to today's woman. Together we develop clothing combinations that allow a woman to feel elegant, confident and highly individual.

To perpetuate the spirit of Dior is to create pure, precisely drawn lines, with defined, perfectly balanced volume, and then underline them with amazing cutting techniques.

Playing with the masculine-feminine also follows the Dior image — the use, for example, of harsher fabrics, like Prince of Wales and hound's-tooth checks. I go beyond the historic

'Alcove' an evening ensemble designed by Gianfranco Ferré for the House of Dior, Autumn-Winter collection 1993–94. The rich colours and motifs of the East inspired this dramatic outfit, made in an unusual combination of mohair and organza.

trademarks of the House of Dior, but by doing so I also reinforce them, using the counterplay of colours like the notes of an organ, an exchange between the contrasts of black and white or the subtler shades of beige and grey.

This return to the source allows me to re-centre, purify or elaborate on my designs as my instinct dictates, and then to re-create a 'truly Dior universe' in conjunction with the staff of this prestigious establishment.

'I have been seduced by this marvellous instrument — Dior's workrooms, design teams and his image. It's as if I had been given a Stradivarius to play on entirely as I wished.'[2]

* *Gianfranco Ferré is Creator of the Haute Couture, Haute Fourrure (Haute Couture Furs), Women's Prêt-à-Porter and Prêt-à-Porter Furs at Christian Dior.*
1. Elie Rabourdin and Alice Chavanne, eds. *Je suis couturier* (I am a couturier), by Christian Dior, Editions du Conquistador, Paris, 1951, p62. **2.** Gianfranco Ferré, cited by François Baudot, 'Gianfranco Ferré', *L'Officiel de la Couture*, April 1989, p182.

Christian Dior: the magic of fashion

by Louise Mitchell*

Throughout the history of French decorative arts and design, there has been a complex relationship between the continuity of French tradition and the spirit of innovation and change. In both form and function, a dialogue has been maintained between innovation and tradition that has given French decorative arts their distinctive appearance and unique history. The success story of Christian Dior and his couture house is representative of this theme in French design.

Before the French Revolution the court was the focal point of the creation and dissemination of style in matters of dress. Traditional values inherited from the ancien régime — fine crafting, respect for luxury materials, and refinement of detail and finish — were integrated into the expanding luxury industries that flourished in nineteenth-century France. After the role of the couturier emerged during the Second Empire (1852–1870), haute couture became stamped on the international consciousness as typically French. The standards of creativity and skill set by designers such as the Callot Soeurs, Poiret, Chanel, Vionnet and Balenciaga in the first half of the twentieth century reinforced Paris's role as the undisputed centre of fashion. By the time of the Second World War, haute couture had proved its monetary and cultural value for France.

Recognition of haute couture's worth as a symbol for France helped set the scene for Christian Dior's extraordinary success when he launched his house in the years immediately after the war. With a disregard for postwar rationing and a conscious effort to revive the spirit of the luxurious fashions of the Second Empire and the *belle époque*, Dior brought excitement back to fashion and revived haute couture. In doing so, he demonstrated not only an outstanding flair for dress design, but also a shrewd understanding of French tradition in the decorative arts and its significance to markets abroad.

The exhibition *Christian Dior: the magic of fashion* is primarily a retrospective of Dior's decade of achievement as the most authoritative figure in the world of fashion. It begins with the 'Bar' suit of 1947, an outfit that encapsulates the New Look, which was to make Dior a household name. It continues with over sixty garments that represent his seasonal collections up to the time of his death in 1957. The exhibition concludes with designs by Dior's successors at the House of Dior: Yves Saint Laurent, Marc Bohan and the present designer, the Italian Gianfranco Ferré. Extending the exhibition up to the present shows the continuity of the Dior tradition and house style.

A publication like this is an opportunity to expand on exhibition themes. The exhibition's storyline was developed by the major lenders, Christian Dior archives and the Union

Française des Arts du Costume (UFAC). The French curators, Marika Genty from the House of Dior and Lydia Kamitsis from UFAC, have highlighted Dior's approach to design in terms of seasonal changes in silhouettes, cut and construction, as well as in the use of opulent fabric embellishments, such as embroidery, that reveal the dazzling technical skills of the Parisian workrooms.

A major section of the exhibition, entitled 'The Dior wardrobe', categorises clothes according to time of day and purpose, which again highlights the tradition of couture recalling court etiquette. The essays by curators Marika Genty and Lydia Kamitsis provide the background to the exhibition approach. Gianfranco Ferré in his essay acknowledges the interplay of tradition and innovation in his collections for the House of Dior and gives credit to the workrooms that realise his designs.

My own contribution has been to look at the influence that French fashion, particularly that of Christian Dior, had in Australia in the postwar years. Because of its relevance to a local audience, a section about the Australian response has been included in the exhibition. Only a year after the New Look was launched, Sydney had the opportunity to view a collection of Dior garments, billed as the first collection to be seen outside France. The collection was shown at David Jones department store in Sydney, one of the many stores around the country

that had considerable interest in promoting French fashion to the Australian buyer. The late 1940s and 1950s was a time of intense interest in Paris fashion, and it was a period when the moderately priced market was flooded with fashion derivative of Paris.

At the heart of Dior's success was his ability to combine the seemingly inconsistent areas of exclusive design and mass merchandising. Christian Dior's business acumen ensured that his house reaped considerable benefits from cooperation with department stores the world over and from his being the first couturier to develop a licensing system. As Lydia Kamitsis points out in her essay, Dior founded a fashion empire on a past that took its strongest guide-lines from the traditions of French *art de vivre*, whilst summoning a new era of couture in which underwriting by the mass market ensured the continuation of the unique and expensive handmade designs of the couturier.

** Louise Mitchell is a curator of Decorative Arts and Design at the Powerhouse Museum, Sydney.*

*Dior mannequins in 1957. For each collection Dior presented about 170 garments in a show
lasting up to two hours. The order of each show was carefully set, beginning with suits,
then formal town dresses, then more formal outfits, cocktail dresses, short evening dresses,
and long evening dresses and ball gowns. The finale would be the wedding dress.
Photo by Loomis Dean, Life Magazine, 1957.*

the

House

of

Christian

Dior

Couture and elegance

by Marika Genty*

'Far from wanting to revolutionise fashion … I only wanted to dress the most elegant women, from the most elegant ranks of society.'[1]

Such boldness from one so timid was enough to convince industrialist Marcel Boussac when Christian Dior came to him with his plan: to create a fashion house under his own name, something 'small and secluded, with very few workrooms; within them the work would be done according to the highest traditions of *haute couture*; … and would be aimed at a clientèle of really elegant women'.[2] It would produce only clothes 'which would give an impression of simplicity, [but] would in fact involve elaborate workmanship'[3] to cater to markets abroad. The die was cast, and on 8 October 1946 the Société Christian Dior was formed.

But just who was the man behind the name Christian Dior? Born in 1905 at Granville in Normandy, Christian Dior did not come to the world of fashion until the age of thirty, after

Opposite: 'Curaçao', from the 1954 Autumn-Winter collection, known as the H-line. Dior's intention was to create an elongated, youthful line by pushing up the bust and dropping the waist to the hip. The press dubbed it the String Bean or Flat Look, mistaking the high bustline for no bust. Photo by Henry Clarke.

13

originally training for a diplomatic career, setting up an art gallery and travelling widely outside France. He worked briefly as a fashion illustrator, but from 1938 to the declaration of the Second World War he was employed as an assistant to couturier Robert Piguet, and then became a junior designer for Lucien Lelong. At Lelong's he learned a sense of fabric, honed his creative talents and observed the workings of a major fashion house.

In 1946 he left Lelong and set up his own premises at 30 avenue Montaigne in 'an attractive dwelling ... with [a] classical and Parisian elegance. I was determined that my décor should not degenerate into elaborate decorations and distract the eye from my clothes.'[4] The pearl grey and white Louis XVI décor he knew from his childhood was perfectly in tune with the atmosphere at his establishment and, in its characteristic elegance, contributed to the famous Dior look.

Such surrounds demanded 'a staff of great class',[5] rigorously handpicked by Christian Dior. His gift lay in his choice of the best employees who, along with the clout of Marcel Boussac, allowed him to develop the quality he strove for as 'a conscientious craftsman'[6] and gave free rein to his imagination.

14

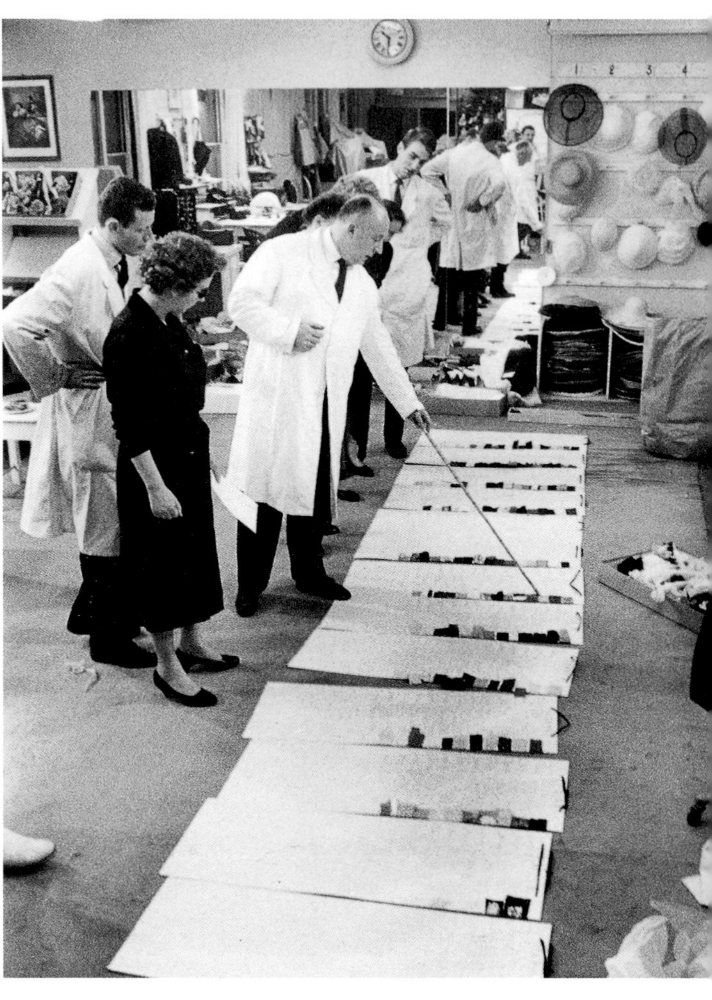

Christian Dior's first collection was unveiled to *le Tout Paris* (the cream of Parisian society) on 12 February 1947, amid great excitement. It was received with 'a hurricane of applause'. 'It's quite a revolution, dear Christian,' said Carmel Snow, chief editor of *Harper's Bazaar*, uttering her famous phrase: 'Your dresses have such a new look. They are wonderful, you know.'[7] And so the New Look, as the first Dior collection came to be known, was born.

Deliberately turning his back on the military style so favoured in the 1940s, Christian Dior revived the feminine look, with clothes that were all soft curves. His dresses emphasised the breasts, featured little rounded shoulders and a nipped-in waist, flaring at the hips into a straight or flowing skirt that dropped to below calf length. These were the new lines *à la Dior*, typified in his 'Bar' suit.

An afternoon dress could take anything from 3 to 40 metres of fabric: 40 metres of faille were used to make 'Chérie'. This abundance of fabric signalled the end of postwar restraint and heralded the kind of fashion women hungered for, and this was the key to the enormous success of the New Look.

On the other side of the Atlantic, however, department stores reacted with hostility after

their orders of Dior gowns sold out in the space of twenty-four hours. Alliances were formed to defend short skirts, and Dior was accused of 'disfiguring' women. Only the strenuous efforts of the fashion editors saved the day, by convincing the buyers to go back to Paris. By the end of 1947 America had been conquered, and Nieman Marcus in Dallas awarded Christian Dior the Oscar of Haute Couture in recognition of the new life he had breathed into fashion.

Orders began to mount up and, to cope with the demand, two new workrooms were added to the three Dior had started with. The second collection was even more successful than the first.

The next step was to expand and take advantage of the Christian Dior name: why not create accessories to his designs, articles like perfume, furs, hats, stockings, gloves, shoes and jewellery? Not even the slightest detail of elegance was to be ignored. Christian Dior's dream was now realised: to dress women 'from head to foot',[8] right down to their underwear.

In order to satisfy Dior's desire to provide a complete wardrobe, a whole network sprang

up around the central hub. Jacques Rouet, Dior's administrative manager and financier, soon put in place a system for manufacture under licence to the name Christian Dior. Licensing contracts were signed with department stores in Australia, Canada, Cuba, Chile and Mexico.

From the earliest days of the couture house, the name of Christian Dior extended its influence beyond its native borders. In 1948 Christian Dior opened boutiques in New York and Caracas, and another followed in London in 1954.

With twenty-eight workrooms by 1954 the Dior empire was flourishing. The future was bright. But every season demanded new designs to surprise his two to three thousand clients and inspire them to renew their Christian Dior wardrobes.

Names of lines like *Zig-Zag*, *Envol* (Flight), *Cyclone*, *Moulins à Vent* (Windmills) or *Ciseaux* (Scissors) not only created an image in the public's mind, but also made movement the focus of each collection. Dior's whirlwind pleated dresses gave life and youth to the form, transforming the wearer into a flower. The Z-shape formed by the folds of a gown recalled the flighty strokes of a pencil sketch. The impression of flight with every step came from an unequal distribution of the fullness of the skirt of a dress.

Creating volume, emphasising a neckline, accentuating a waist with an overlay, a bow or a crossover, asymmetrical effect — to assiduous followers of the seasonal collections these were the details of the broad direction in which Christian Dior was moving, keeping the New Look well and truly alive.

But were these details and seasonal changes enough to entice women to wear Dior? They were also invited to dream a little with embroidered gowns rich in Persian-inspired motifs and equal to the finest pieces of jewellery. And tempted to reconsider the charms of a rustic ball with dresses sewn with daisies, currants or dragonflies. Creating an embossed effect, creating texture with lace, braid or jet — anything to fuel women's imaginations.

Each collection was a cunningly orchestrated *coup de théâtre*: by constantly coming up with something new Dior ensured maximum publicity for every collection.

After the wasp waist and oversized full skirts, Christian Dior realised that women wanted clothes that were in tune with the demands of daily life. He moved away from the New Look and onto collections dominated by geometric lines. In the 1950s the words 'vertical', 'oblique', 'oval' and 'long' came up time and time again, suggesting a stylisation of the female figure. But the culmination of Dior's geometric lines were the *H*, *A* and *Y* designs.

The *H-line*, created for the 1954 Autumn-Winter collection, essentially lengthened and streamlined the torso to create a half-girl/half-woman effect. The dresses, suits and coats were cut along parallel lines like the letter H. The Flat Look or Haricot Vert (String Bean), as the fashion media dubbed them, seemed to flatten the chest — arousing a great deal of criticism and controversy.

The shape symbolised by the letter A, introduced in the Spring-Summer collection of 1955, was similar in construction to the *H-line*, but was based on two joining diagonals. The dominant effect was once again a longer torso, while the crossbar of the A, representing the waist, was more mobile.

The *Y-line* of the 1955 Autumn-Winter collection was a reaction against long basques and dropped waists. In this collection the two upward strokes of the Y formed a wide, high bustline. The waist was tightly nipped in and placed higher than usual, giving an extra length to the skirt, and therefore also to the legs. The key element in Dior's letter collections was the variation in waistlines.

But closer to Dior's heart than the latest novelty was his desire to meet the needs of his elegant clientele. He developed a system of *chartes* (charts) to ensure balance in the collections and to give an overview of the types of garments each one featured. These large sheets of paper (measuring 24 x 19 inches) were pinned to the wall or placed on the floor of his studio and detailed every item in the collection, from suits to evening wear, in thirteen different categories. A fabric sample for each garment was attached, along with any relevant

For Dior the hat was an indispensable part of the total look, complementing the proportions and line of the dress. He spent many hours designing and selecting hats for each of his outfits, and his hat styles came to be as influential as his clothes. Photo by Louise Dahl-Wolfe, 1953.

Right: On the day of the showing of a new collection, chaos reigned as dressers, mannequins, hairdressers and workroom heads crowded into the dressing-rooms. For Dior, this was the moment when the collection passed out of his hands into those of the mannequins. Here the mannequin is being dressed in 'May', an evening gown from Dior's Spring-Summer 1953 collection. Photo by Henri Cartier-Bresson, 1953.

Left: Seamstresses at work at Maison Dior. When Dior set up his house he carefully handpicked his staff, aiming for a mix of technical expertise with inspirational flair. His seamstresses in particular had to be technically very skilled: each dress was constructed on a foundation, and, instead of using darts, Dior insisted that they mould the fabric to shape with hot irons. Photo by Bellini.

Presented in his Envol (Flight) collection of 1948, Dior considered the 'Adelaïde' evening gown his masterpiece. With 70 metres of tulle in the skirt alone the dress embodies the femininity, luxury and extravagance of Dior's New Look and marks the end of wartime restraint. It was shown at the Dior parade in Sydney in 1948. Photo by Coffin, 1948.

Olivia de Havilland was a long-standing customer of Dior. At her wedding to Pierre Galante she wore the 'A' suit from Dior's Spring-Summer 1955 collection. Photo by Mike Dulmen.

instructions for the workrooms making up the pattern. The chart also featured the names of the individual models and the mannequins who wore them at the collections.

The Dior charts have been preserved in the company's archives and are considered an invaluable legacy. They are evidence of the detailed nature of the lines created by Christian Dior and his successors and, even more importantly, they constitute a resource through which we can more readily identify each of their designs.

After the devastating death of Christian Dior on 24 October 1957, Yves Saint Laurent was asked to take over the studio. He was only twenty-one years old, but Dior had already identified him as crown prince. Saint Laurent's first collection, in 1958, went under the name *Trapèze* (Trapezium). It was a triumph, and for three years he continued Dior's geometric themes. But by 1960, quite soon after his departure, a new spirit had taken over.

Marc Bohan took another tack when it came to feminine elegance: he wanted distinctiveness without rigidity, and sought to make Dior products more accessible. Two prêt-à-porter (ready-to-wear) lines were introduced: Miss Dior in 1967 and Christian Dior Monsieur in 1970.

From the early 1950s Dior began to move away from the nipped waists and full skirts of the New Look, and his collections became dominated by geometric lines. His Y-line was clearly expressed in 'Voyageur' (Voyager) from the Autumn-Winter 1955 collection. The large stole creates the arms of the Y and the slim skirt the stem. Photo by Willy Maywald, 1955.

In 1968 Frédéric Castet joined Bohan with the launch of Dior's couture furs. The harmonious assembly of shapes and lines, the variety and combination of furs, the ingenious preparation of the hides, new colours, and work with the best workrooms added a new dynamism. So many great talents under the one roof played an important part in carrying on the name and spreading the reputation of the House of Dior.

Since 1989 Gianfranco Ferré has continued the Dior spirit. His emphasis is on geometric and graphic designs, the purest lines and masculine fabrics, rendered feminine with accentuated curves, and highlighted with lace or organza, embroidery or flowers. His work is a series of colourful and extravagant variations on the abiding theme of the House of Dior: Couture and Elegance.

* *Marika Genty is librarian-archivist for Christian Dior, Paris.*

1. Christian Dior, *Dior by Dior*, translated by Antonia Fraser, Penguin Books, Harmondsworth, 1958, p20 and p135. **2.** Dior, pp7–8. **3.** Dior, p8. **4.** Dior, p19. **5.** Dior, p11. **6.** Dior, p21. **7.** Cited in Françoise Giroud, *Dior: Christian Dior 1905–57*, Thames and Hudson, London, 1987, p9. **8.** Dior, p146.

Christian Dior: a new era in haute couture

by Lydia Kamitsis*

Of all the great names to have made their mark on the history of fashion, only a few have succeeded in doing what Christian Dior did: reinvent the rules, for all time, in the space of a single decade.

With an acute awareness of the importance of his trade, he opened the House of Dior in 1946 and established a way of working that was to signal the advent of a new era in haute couture.

This success story is all the more dazzling because the road that led to it was so long and unusual. Son of an industrialist, Christian Dior had to renounce his artistic leanings to study political science, in accordance with his father's ambitions. But far from thinking of a future diplomatic career, the young student preferred to lead the life of a gilded Bohemian, surrounded by the artist friends who formed his tastes. In 1928, pushed into practising a trade, he obtained (not without difficulty) financial assistance from his parents to open an art gallery, on the express condition that he remain a silent partner. He and his associate, Jacques Bonjean, exhibited the work of artists they admired — Picasso, Braque, Matisse,

Opposite: The 'Bar' suit was a star attraction of Dior's first collection in 1947. The short, fabric-skimping dresses and masculine silhouette of wartime fashions were swept away by the long, full skirts, softly rounded shoulders and tightly nipped waists of the New Look. Photo by Willy Maywald, 1955.

Dufy — and those who were close to them, including Christian Bérard, Salvador Dali and Max Jacob. But this experiment, which satisfied Dior's keen interest in art in all its forms, was cut short by his father's bankruptcy in 1931. He withdrew the funds given by his parents from the gallery, but continued, with his friend Pierre Colle, to promote the Surrealists and Salvador Dali. In 1934 Dior fell ill with tuberculosis and spent a year in convalescence.

On returning to Paris in search of something to satisfy his own needs and help his family, and on the advice of his friends, Dior tried his hand at fashion design. A complete novice, he knew nothing of this world, but a few couturiers, and milliners especially, accepted his sketches, as did the newspapers, including the women's pages of the daily *Le Figaro*.

These hesitant beginnings in fashion took a more decisive turn in 1938 when Robert Piguet hired him as an assistant designer. For the inexperienced Christian Dior, it was an opening into the profession of design, and he was quick to prove his ability. The 'Café Anglais' model he created there attracted a great deal of attention, as did the 'Robes Amphores', and they both showed the essence of what was to become the Dior style. 'Café Anglais', a black-and-white hound's-tooth check suit, consisted of a wide overskirt draped over a full petticoat, and a short, fitted jacket in black woollen fabric. The 'Robes Amphores' featured a full skirt (seemingly inadvertently inverted, so that the skirt's fullness was at the waist rather than the hem), caught in at the waist by a belt — launching the fashion for fuller, rounded hips.

From 1941 Christian Dior spent five years with Lucien Lelong, which gave him the opportunity to perfect his technical knowledge and to develop his sense of discipline in execution. He thus added his skills as a tailor to his talents as a connoisseur, his love of avant-garde art and his proven entrepreneurial ability.

A fortuitous meeting with industrialist Marcel Boussac gave Dior the chance to capitalise on his multifaceted experiences. Drawing on that experience in their new venture — the creation of a fashion house — helped lend originality to what came to be a successful business enterprise. From the time of his first collection, presented in February 1947, Christian Dior reaffirmed his unfailing ability to create an event. He captured the spirit of the times — and ultimately created it.

In a reaction to what he called the 'hideous fashions'[1] that had characterised the war years, Dior chose to take an opposing perspective. He said that 'Hats were far too large, skirts far too short, jackets far too long'[2] and replaced them with the exact opposite. He proposed a feminine image, one contrary to the military look. Novel though it seemed, this merely harked back to the age of the crinoline. The New Look, with its rounded shoulders, wasp waists, generous hips and long, full skirts was only new from a very short view of fashion history. It was a stroke of genius to pass off as innovation what a whole century had

'Diorama', the centrepiece of Dior's second collection, for Autumn-Winter 1947, had taken Dior's seamstresses 230 hours to complete and included 26 metres of fabric and 42 metres of braid. Photo by Forlano.

done its utmost to forget. It appears that the success of this style was chiefly due to the persistent need that people seem to have in times of crisis to seek comfort in the trappings of what are thought to have been more carefree times. After years of deprivation and misery, the wish to believe in a bright future pushed people to a desire for splendour. Dior sensed this and accentuated it in his second collection. 'Dresses took up fantastic yardages of material, and this time went right down to the ankles ... A golden age seemed to have come again ... What did the weight of my sumptuous materials, my heavy velvets and brocades, matter? When hearts were light, mere fabrics could not weigh the body down. Abundance was still much too much of a novelty for a poverty cult to develop out of inverted snobbism.'[3]

The passion for opulence inherent in the quantity of the materials and in the variety of embroideries and accessories was to be the best way of restoring the tradition of French haute couture.

The success of such ideas, and the clever management of the spin-offs they generated, enabled Dior to make luxury a serious business, a rationally organised industry. His direct involvement in the business side of the House of Dior took haute couture out of the undoubtedly brilliant, but limited, domain of a very small élite and offered it to the world, turning haute couture into a financial empire. He analysed his role thus: 'We are merchants

Each parade closed with the announcement 'Grand Mirage' and a mannequin would emerge in a wedding dress. 'Fidelité' (Fidelity) was shown in the Autumn-Winter 1949 collection. Photo by Willy Maywald.

*Opposite: 'Mexique' (Mexico) from the Autumn-Winter 1951 collection. Dior's favourite, the **Longue** (Long) line marked the waistline under the bust, giving the illusion of a high waist and a long body line. Photo by Louise Dahl-Wolfe, 1951.*

of ideas. Each season we have a certain stock of ideas to sell. Then we have to analyse, in a strictly commercial manner, just what they cost to produce and how many are actually sold.'[4] These ideas rapidly snowballed into the creation of a multitude of products: stockings, gloves, ties, perfumes and shoes bearing the label of the house, and bringing to fruition the dream to dress a woman in Christian Dior from head to foot.

Dior was a determined innovator: in 1947 he hit on the idea of establishing a boutique that would offer a choice of accessories such as jewellery, flowers and scarves. In 1948 he diversified by launching a range of simpler dresses that were more modest than those of the main collection. The idea of a boutique collection was born, opening the way to what was later to become a common practice among couturiers. Other items were added — gifts and even light furniture — necessitating a move in 1955 from the tiny boutique at 30 avenue Montaigne to larger premises at 15 rue François 1er. The décor of the new boutique reflected the Dior style perfectly. The couturier had entrusted the task to Victor Grandpierrre, who re-created the spirit of the Louis XVI style that was so dear to Dior, but with a 'very 1955' *belle époque* flavour.

Christian Dior based his universe on a past whose strongest references came from the French *art de vivre* (the splendours of Louis XVI, the imperial feasts of the Second Empire, the frivolity of the *belle époque*). But far from dwelling on the past, he drew from it the essence of

PLAN DE TURGOT
1734-1739
AVERTISSEMENT
PLAN
VILLE L'EVEQUE
FAUBOURG SAINT

Right: Twice each year Dior presented his collections to a select group of private customers, buyers and the press. At this opening of the Autumn-Winter 1955 collection Marlene Dietrich is seated in the front row. Photo by Willy Maywald, 1955.

Left: For Dior, accessories were an important part of creating a total look and his dream was to be able to dress women from head to toe. These are his New Look accessories of 1948. Photo by Frank Scherschel, Life Magazine

Dior selected each of his house mannequins personally. He believed that it was their style and personality that brought his clothes to life. Here he is pictured with Renée, of whom he said 'Of all my mannequins, Renée is probably the one who comes nearest to my ideal. Every dress she puts on seems to be a success as though there existed an exact equivalence between her proportions and those of my imagination' (Dior by Dior, page 128). Photo by Henry Clarke, 1957.

The opening of the Théâtre du Château de Groussay, 1957. From left: Patricia Lopez-Willshaw wearing 'Festival' from Dior's Autumn-Winter 1956 collection, her husband Arturo, Francine Weisweiller wearing 'Muguet' (Lily-of-the-valley) from the Spring-Summer 1957 collection, Edouard Dermit and Jean Cocteau. Photo by André Ostier.

a world that he made his own and put forward as the epitome of good taste and elegance. His cleverly coordinated collections conjured up the rather paradoxical image of a modern woman, free of any financial constraints, yet enjoying a demanding and active social life.

The range and subtle variations of a Dior wardrobe made it the arbiter of a new code of good taste, the privilege of a happy few. But, even more importantly, the seasonal need to create something new brought about the stereotype of the style-setter. By launching a new line that was in seeming contrast to the preceding look, Dior turned the very notion of fashion (that of the passing craze) into a system ruled by its own dictates. Never before had the fear of being *démodée* (out of fashion) reached such a high proportion of women. Take the example of the sort of advice that appeared in numerous magazines the day after the explosive appearance of the New Look. To readers who could never aspire to owning a real Dior, *Elle*'s October 1947 issue suggested clever solutions for shortening jackets and lengthening skirts, to rescue dresses already in their readers' wardrobes.

The collections, analysed in advance in a program accompanying each presentation, bore names that sounded like so many slogans. Everything was determined — the colours and fabrics — down to the smallest accessories. The 'total look' that Dior invented was destined to create a lasting career, for himself and his colleagues. He had the undeniable qualities of a fashion designer and businessman, but also (although he denied it) the instincts of a good

publicist. His much-imitated programs are an example of this. The creed of the creator, his intentions, his vision are clearly exposed, leaving the commentators only a small margin for personal analysis. He was inclined to be both an attentive observer of his work, and his own critic, which became apparent in the publication of his two autobiographical books in 1951 and 1956. These were also professions of faith regarding his trade, which came to symbolise, thanks to him, not only the dream of great luxury, but also that of commercial success.

Although Dior was terrified of the idea of travel, he was astute enough to understand the primary importance of direct contact with the vast world he had to conquer. America, incarnation of modernity, appeared to him as the land of possibility towards which he had to turn. In 1948 he decided to open a shop for a deluxe *prêt-à-porter* (ready-to-wear) fashion house producing designs adapted for the American market. This great first in the history of haute couture was followed by other similar initiatives, scattering the Dior label to the four corners of the globe and consolidating the prestige of his empire of luxury.

In less than a decade, he had established the ground rules for the renaissance of French couture. Owing to his rigorous adherence to the rules of his craft and his extraordinary flair, fashion even became a respectable subject outside the fashion houses. On 3 August 1954, the Sorbonne invited Christian Dior to present a lecture titled the 'Aesthetics of fashion' in a course on the history of French civilisation.

The formal afternoon dress 'Zerline'

was part of Dior's Autumn-Winter

1957 collection, the last

collection he would present.

Photo by Willy Maywald, 1957.

Now deemed an heir to the great figures of fashion whom he admired — Poiret, Chanel, Vionnet — the art lover, now couturier, could claim his legacy and combine their qualities. To the flamboyant side of Paul Poiret, he linked the luxury of simplicity dear to Gabrielle Chanel and the advanced techniques of Madeleine Vionnet, adding his own innate sense of construction and quality of execution.

In a few concise phrases he once summed up the challenge confronting the field to which he gave a modern face: 'Fashion has its own moral code however frivolous: ... The maintenance of the tradition of fashion is in the nature of an act of faith. In a century which attempts to tear the heart out of every mystery, fashion guards its secret well, and is the best possible proof that there is still magic abroad.'[5] He concluded, with clairvoyance, that 'the great adventure which constitutes Parisian couture is not merely a Temple of Vanities: it is a charming outward manifestation of an ancient civilisation, which intends to survive'.[6]

* *Lydia Kamitsis is curator of the Union Française des Arts du Costume, Paris.*
1. Christian Dior, *Dior by Dior*, translated by Antonia Fraser, Penguin Books, Harmondsworth, 1958, p4. **2.** Dior, p4. **3.** Dior, p33. **4.** Dior, Elie Rabourdin and Alice Chavanne, eds. *Je suis couturier* (I am a couturier), by Christian Dior, Editions du Conquistador, Paris, 1951, p118. **5.** Dior, pp189–90. **6.** Dior, p190.

Christian Dior with the mannequin Sylvie. Two months before Dior started designing,
the fabric merchants brought their samples for him to make a selection. Wearing the linen
toile, or pattern, of the dress, mannequins would stand for hours while
Dior draped fabrics over them. Photo by Bellini.

Christian Dior and 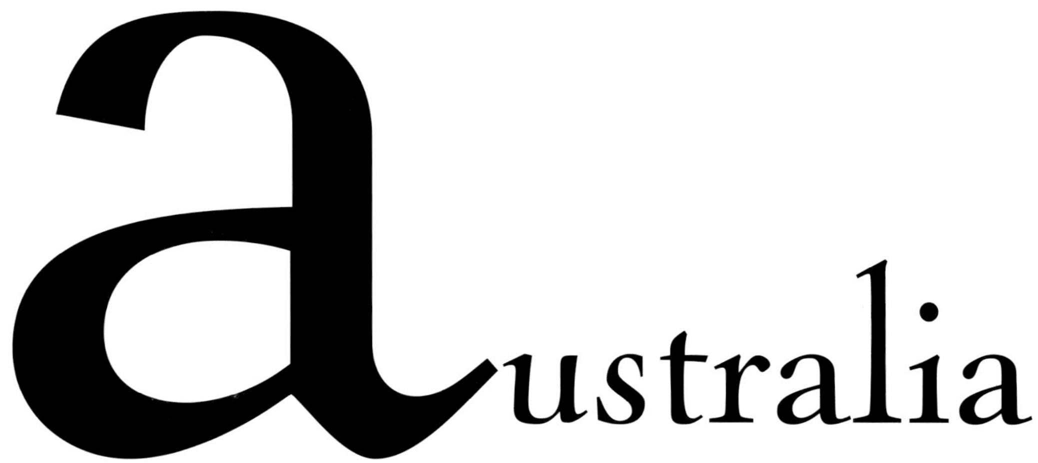 *Australia*

by Louise Mitchell*

Mention Christian Dior to Australians with memories of the postwar years, and they are likely to recall the excitement of seeing the New Look after years of wartime austerity. The success of Dior's New Look sparked the revival of haute couture, and his authoritative word made headline news both in France and abroad. The postwar period was a time of intense interest in French fashion and Australia became part of an international audience that played an important role in the making of 'French style'.

Despite the distance, Australia was by no means isolated from the influence of Paris. Communication and travel improved dramatically after the war and, through the efforts of the fashion media, department stores and the couture houses, those Australians interested in fashion were able to keep a close eye on Paris couture, particularly the House of Dior. It was no longer necessary to go to Paris to purchase fashion: fashion came to the buyer, not only through the press and publicity, but also through the boutiques opened in cities across the world and beyond the fashion centres of Paris, New York and London.

Opposite: One Australian photographer who successfully captured the allure of French fashion was Athol Shmith, who was commissioned to do a series of fashion shots, including this one of Patricia 'Bambi' Tuckwell in a Dior cocktail dress in 1949.

To a great extent, the couture-led recovery of Paris can be credited to the intense competitive interest of department stores and fashion magazines around the world. Fashion editors and buyers flocked to Paris in the postwar years. The most important market for France was the United States, whose interest was particularly stimulated by the *Théâtre de la Mode* of 1945, a travelling exhibition of child-size dolls made of wire armatures with porcelain heads, dressed by Parisian couture houses and mounted on sets designed by famous artists. Organised by the Chambre Syndicale de la Couture Parisienne as part of a carefully planned strategy of the French Ministry of Reconstruction, the purpose of the *Théâtre de la Mode* was to reassert the dominance of French fashion over, and define it against, American fashion, which had developed considerably during the period of isolation from Europe. The French had quickly come to understand that their own fashion industry had suffered little from the war in comparison with the devastation wreaked on French heavy industries. For although fashion, to some, was trivial, it nonetheless represented hope to France after four years of German occupation. By attracting buyers back to Paris, the *Théâtre de la Mode* paved the way for the reception of Dior's New Look in early 1947.

Unlike the United States, which had developed its own fashion industry during the war, Australia needed little encouragement to be enticed back to Paris. The interest in and

In 1957 David Jones, in association with the Australian Women's Weekly *brought a parade of Dior couture originals to Australia. This cover depicts the seven Dior house mannequins who came to Australia.*

Opposite: Christian Dior showing his house mannequins Australia on the globe in preparation for the 1957 Dior parade. Dior and his staff often wore overalls while working. Photo by André Gandner.

prestige of French style had been set during the interwar years and was to be intensified after the war. Before the war, Australian women interested in fashion had kept abreast of the Parisian image of the modern woman through foreign fashion magazines and local publications, such as *The Home*. For those who could afford it, French fashion could be purchased through upmarket local dressmaking establishments, which were as French as their owners could make them — bearing French names and often run by French people. Since the 1920s, however, for the vast majority of middle-class Australian women, the preferred choice had been the department store, with its ready-made merchandise. Again, Paris was the inspiration for department stores such as Sydney's Mark Foys, which was modelled after Paris's Bon Marché, and David Jones's new store, which opened in 1927. David Jones was particularly noted for its sophisticated and modern window displays, fashion parades and the French salon, where shoppers could select from a glamorous array of ready-made gowns.

During the war Australian women had little exposure to Paris and its fashion industry. In the early 1940s, the main source of fashion influence was the United States. Rationing, which regulated the amount of clothing available to Australian women, was introduced in 1942. Government war restrictions also necessitated the simplification of civilian clothing, which was aimed at economising on both materials and labour. The resulting style of dress

had a simple, austere silhouette, with square, padded shoulders and a short, narrow skirt. Reflecting in 1957 on his New Look designs compared with wartime fashions, Christian Dior wrote: 'In December 1946, as a result of the war and uniforms, women still looked and dressed like Amazons. But I designed clothes for flower-like women, with rounded shoulders, full feminine busts, and handspan waists above enormous spreading skirts.'[1]

Australians were able to renew their admiration of French fashion as early as 1946 through a series of fashion parades organised by the country's leading women's magazine, the *Australian Women's Weekly*. Known as the French Fashion Parades, the idea for the parades came from Mary Hordern, wife of businessman Anthony Hordern IV. Mary's sister Gretel had married Frank Packer, owner of the *Australian Women's Weekly*, where Mary worked as a fashion editor. With Frank Packer's financial backing, Mary Hordern pursued her project with enthusiasm, travelling to Paris, meeting designers, selecting gowns and accessories, and recruiting mannequins, a fashion director and a parade technician. The logistics of it all were complex and novel, and the project made good copy. Mary's movements were assiduously reported on by the *Weekly*, as the opportunity to see French fashion so soon after the war had captured the public imagination.

The first *Australian Women's Weekly* French Fashion Parade was launched with a gala

The Australian Women's Weekly's *fashion advisor, Mary Hordern, snapped with Christian Dior, 'the newest designer in Paris'. Photo by Jean-Louis Moussempes, 1947.*

Opposite: Geiger's, an up-market fashion accessory shop in Collins Street, Melbourne, commissioned Wolfgang Sievers to photograph the French mannequins recruited in 1946 for the Australian Women's Weekly *first French Fashion Parade. Photo by Wolfgang Sievers, 1946.*

opening in David Jones's Great Restaurant and was reported as one of the most glamorous events of the year. It consisted of gowns from the houses of Patou, Lanvin, Lelong, Molyneux, Balmain, Carven and Fath. Similar gala openings were held at Myer's Mural Hall in Melbourne, Myer in Adelaide and at Finney Isles in Brisbane. Although the fashions were not for sale, the stores were able to produce credible copies for purchase.

The success of the parades took Mary Hordern back to Paris the following year to organise more. On this second trip she met Christian Dior, who had only just become famous, and had her picture taken with him for the *Weekly*.[3] Christian Dior, she assured her *Weekly* readers, was 'the' name in Paris and she was determined to feature his designs in the parade. A Dior New Look black cocktail dress in the parade was illustrated in the *Weekly*, and a pattern was provided so readers could run up their own version at home.

Like the previous year's parade, the 1947 *Weekly* parade consisted of couture clothes from a variety of Parisian houses. Again French mannequins were recruited and flown to Australia by Lancastrian plane (a gruelling sixty hours, with numerous stopovers). A change of venue from David Jones to Mark Foys underscores local rivalries.[2] In the same year David Jones launched its Paris Fashions for All policy with a selection of fashions, including some from Dior, which were reproduced in the store's Marlborough Street workroom so that Australian

women could enjoy the 'luxury and glamour of Paris high fashion and at prices to suit all pockets'. Later in the year, the store invited the Paris designer Pierre Balmain to Sydney to lecture on fashion and to design clothes specifically for 'the Australian woman'. The underlying assumption of the store's new policy was that it was every Australian woman's dream to own a creation from a Paris couture house.

In 1948 David Jones was able to upstage the competition by persuading Christian Dior to agree to the first-ever parade of his New Look clothes in Australia. In April the *Herald*'s London-based fashion editor reported that David Jones's spring parade would show 'the first-ever representative collection of original fashions designed by Christian Dior to be shown outside of Paris'.[3] When the parade arrived, the *Herald* headlines claimed Dior's 'tiny waists and whirlaway skirts cause sensation'.[4] The parade was launched in August and emphasised the designer's current silhouette, *Envol* (Flight) and *Zig-Zag*. Australian mannequins approximating the Dior house mannequins modelled the clothes. Dior lent himself to the occasion through an interview with the *Herald*'s European correspondent. Dior claimed Australia was the right country for his clothes as 'living in the sunshine of a comparatively new country unscathed by war, Australians have a cleaner, brighter outlook and are more receptive to new ideas than the tired people of European countries.'[5]

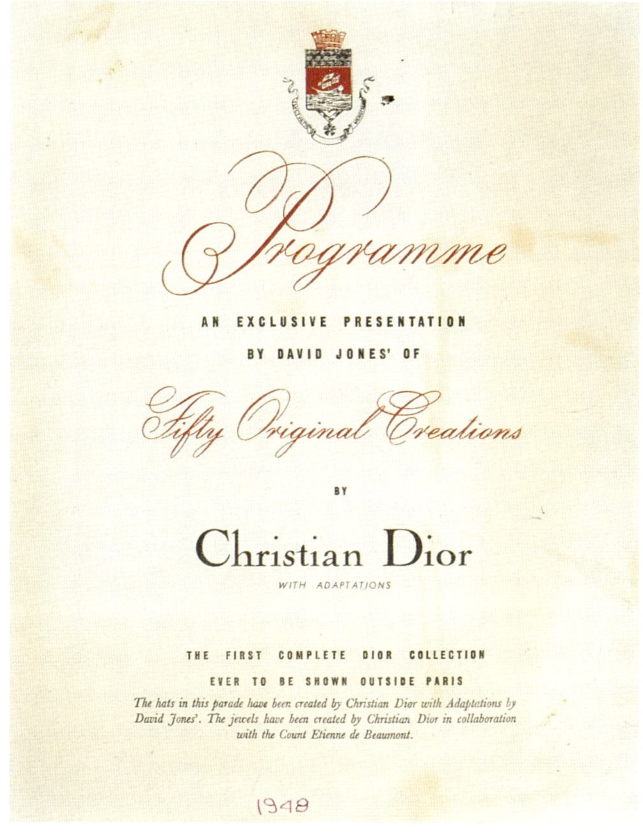

Opposite: Invitation to David Jones's French fashion parade. Launched in 1947, David Jones's Paris Fashions for All policy aimed to provide copies of Paris couture to suit all pockets.

Program for the parade held at David Jones in 1948. The program reveals that a selection of Australian-made copies were modelled alongside the original garments.

The Dior clothes at the David Jones parade were worn by local mannequins, but the *Australian Women's Weekly* parades were able to get extensive publicity through their recruitment of French mannequins. For the four years in succession that the parades were staged, Mary Hordern interviewed and selected four mannequins to travel to Australia to model the clothes. By all accounts, the reception the French women received when they arrived in Australia was overwhelming.

Paule Paulus, originally a Dior model and now living in Melbourne, travelled to Australia in 1948 with the *Weekly* show and recalled that she was encouraged to come here by a mannequin from the previous year's parade. If a woman called Mary Hordern approached her to go to Australia she was to accept at once, for 'Australians' said her compatriot, 'were absolutely crazy'.[6] Apart from the endless stories in the *Weekly* about their flawless complexions, hair colour, accents and charming personalities, the French mannequins received coverage in most newspapers and radio stations throughout Australia. Fêted as international celebrities, the women received the red-carpet treatment, reflecting the aura of glamour and prestige French femininity had in Australia in the postwar years.

The sexual allure and sophisticated style of French femininity as fashioned by Dior was projected through fashion photographs of the time. With the upsurge in production of

A group of leading Australian mannequins were carefully selected to model Christian Dior clothes in the 1948 David Jones parade. June Dally-Watkins, seen here and opposite modelling in the Christian Dior parades, recalls that a major prerequisite was having an eighteen inch waist to fit into the Dior garments. Photo right by Bowen.

consumer goods and the expansion of department store chains after the war, fashion photography was increasingly in demand, as it was used both in catalogues and for window displays. A local photographer who demonstrated a flair for capturing the look that embraced the modern Paris style was Melbourne fashion photographer Athol Shmith. When the French mannequins arrived in Melbourne in 1948, Athol Shmith was commissioned by Myers department store to photograph them.

Shmith portrayed the mannequins as being totally removed from ordinary people. The opulence and contrived glamour so characteristic of French fashion of this period is portrayed in his portrait of Madame Chamberlaine, director of the French parades in 1947 and 1948. An equally memorable photograph by Shmith is a portrait of the Australian model Patricia 'Bambi' Tuckwell wearing a dramatic Dior New Look black dress.

In a recent reflection on her modelling days, Patricia Tuckwell described the 'exhilaration which came with swishing about in those full-skirted, tiny-waisted, many-petticoated garments after the dullness and limitation of wartime clothes'.[7] Such self-gratification was shared by many women, who quickly adopted the New Look, and her comment highlights the excitement Dior brought to fashion.

One of the extraordinary aspects of the New Look was the speed with which it was

assimilated and redefined. There was a ready reception of the New Look in Australia, particularly when compared with England. There was very little hostility to its introduction, and almost none of the moralising about rationing that was experienced in Europe, where war had had a more profound effect.

The sheer prestige of Paris contributed to the New Look's success. Everything to do with Paris fashion seemed to be of interest to Australian women, who eagerly read articles about the hands that sewed the dresses, the mannequins who modelled them and the couturiers who designed them. Local dressmakers cashed in on the prestige of French fashion by modelling themselves on French workrooms. At the upper end of the market, there were the Sydney salons of Germaine Rocher, Madame Pellier and the milliner Henriette Lamotte, while Melbourne had La Petite and Lillian Whiteman's Le Louvre in the 'Paris end' of Collins Street.

The House of Dior was able to build its empire by catering to the needs of retailers. In financial terms the international buyers were Dior's most important clients, since they paid a surcharge of 40–50 per cent on each garment they bought, by which they acquired the right to make copies. They bought the garment without trying it on, often in the form of a toile or a paper pattern.

One of the first to obtain rights to copy and mass produce Dior originals was Douglas Cox of Melbourne, who launched a range of clothes under the label 'Dior, Australia' in June 1949. The style was also rapidly mass produced by middle market firms, such as Adelyn and Curzon's, along with many of the larger department stores.

Most of the Australian-made copies were modified to suit local conditions. This usually meant a toning down of the styles seen in Paris, as there was a widespread view that the exaggerated Paris fashions had to be adapted to suit the ordinary Australian woman. For example, Berlei, another Australian firm that rapidly responded to the influence of the New Look, urged its clients to adopt a policy of 'intelligent frocking'. Berlei produced its Parisian Waist Girdle, a modified version of the *guêpière* worn by Dior mannequins to achieve the then-fashionable 18-inch waist. The firm thought it was 'unlikely that the good sense of Australian women will allow them to follow these extreme couturiers' attempts so slavishly that they will be compelled to wear constricting foundation garments to achieve it ... as Australian women are not sensation seekers, and like to live a healthy, normal, busy life.'[8]

The 1948 Christian Dior parade at the Sydney department store David Jones featured his New Look collection. Opposite: Publicity photo for the 1948 David Jones Dior parade.

SYDNEY
SYDNEY
SYDNEY
DJC 1044/3
DAVID JONES NEWS
Just arrived by air from Paris
Christian Dior's
Fabulous Models
to be shown
JULY 31st
at
DAVID JONES
NSW
TU-784

Another way to purchase a Dior design was through the licensing system, which many Parisian couture houses introduced during the late 1940s and 1950s. The licensing system was initiated by the House of Dior in 1948, when it diversified by opening a branch in New York to sell luxury ready-to-wear goods. From the early 1950s, the House of Dior was responsible for 55 per cent of the entire exports of the French couture houses. Two collections each year were created for American women, and in 1952 an agreement was signed with the House of Youth in Sydney, granting exclusive reproduction rights for Dior's New York ready-to-wear designs. Again these were modified versions of French style. As put by the director of Dior's Australian licensee, 'The prestige attached to the Dior label means a great deal to us, and women need not be frightened of any extreme styles in our Dior collection.'

Christian Dior also collaborated with local manufacturers by using Australian fabric in his clothes. In 1951 a selection of Dior clothes, worn by leading Australian mannequin Judy Barraclough, were shown at the Art Gallery of New South Wales. They were the first imports made by the fashion house in an Australian fabric, a wool jersey by Austral Swiss Textiles Ltd. In this way, the promotion of French fashion in Australia was tied in with the promotion of a burgeoning Australian fashion industry. The Australian Wool Bureau played a

Dior house mannequin Paule Paulus parades for Doe Avedon (left) and Carmel
Snow, the influential American editor-in-chief of Harper's Bazaar. *It was*
she who dubbed Dior's first collection the New Look. Paule Paulus later toured
with the Australian Women's Weekly's *French fashion parades in Australia*
in 1948 and 1949. Photo by Richard Avedon, 1947.

pivotal role by publicising the use of Australian wool by local companies in their production of French copies.

From 1948 onwards there was constant whispering in the press that the great man himself was to visit Australia. Such was his continuing significance that David Jones, in association with the *Australian Women's Weekly*, again negotiated with the House of Dior to bring a major parade of Dior couture originals to Australia in late 1957. Despite Christian Dior's sudden death in October at the age of fifty-two, it was decided to go ahead with the show. Eighty-three outfits from his last collection, *Libre* (Free), were shown in Australia, worn by seven of Dior's house mannequins. The mannequins and parade were supervised in Australia by Madame Suzanne Luling, Dior's sales and staff manager.

The 1957 parade featured the luxurious and glamorous evening dresses for which Dior was famous, along with a new day dress, the chemise, a loose-fitting, unwaisted garment that was the exact opposite of his fitted New Look collection. Originally a Balenciaga creation, the chemise (or sack) was a popular and youthful alternative to the formality of previous Paris designs and proved a forecast of future styles as more and more fashion responded to influences from youth and popular culture.

Christian Dior died at a time when the intense interest in fashion, and in particular in haute couture, was beginning to wane. Australian department stores continued to stage fashion parades, but they were nothing like the lavish productions seen in the late 1940s. The dictatorial voice of the French couture houses was undermined by the new pluralism in dress that gathered force at the end of the fifties. However, the extraordinary achievement of Dior ensured that everyone remembered him. Such was the interest in Christian Dior that two years after his death a local magazine commented that 'The name of Dior is a household word. Those who are interested in fashion may have heard of Balenciaga, Cardin or Balmain, but you don't have to be interested in fashion to have heard about Dior. His New Look has become as famous as the Battle of Waterloo or Lindberg's first Atlantic crossing.'[10]

** Louise Mitchell is a curator of Decorative Arts and Design at the Powerhouse Museum, Sydney.* **1.** Christian Dior, *Dior by Dior*, Penguin Books, Harmondsworth, 1958, p21. **2.** See Valerie Lawson, *Connie Sweetheart: the story of Connie Robertson*, Heinemann, Melbourne, 1990, pp277–9. **3.** 'Christian Dior models for Sydney' by Elene Foster, London fashion writer, *Sydney Morning Herald*, 19 April 1948, p3. **4.** 'Tiny waists and whirlaway skirts cause sensation', *Sydney Morning Herald*, 2 August 1948, p5. **5.** 'New Look Dior calls us representative', Elene Foster, *Sydney Morning Herald*, 27 April 1948, p5. **6.** Interview with Paule Paulus, Melbourne, 13 August 1993. **7.** Correspondence with the Countess of Harewood, 1 October 1993. **8.** 'The New Look and foundations', *Draper of Australasia*, 28 February 1948, p42. **9.** *Sydney Morning Herald*, 15 November 1951, p13. **10.** 'The tyranny of the haughty couture', *Flair,* May 1959, p32.

*This photograph of French fashion is given an Australian flavour with
local mannequin Judy Barraclough posed wearing a Dior model from Madame
Pellier at a cricket match with Test stars Keith Miller, Ian Johnson and
Graeme Hole in the background.*

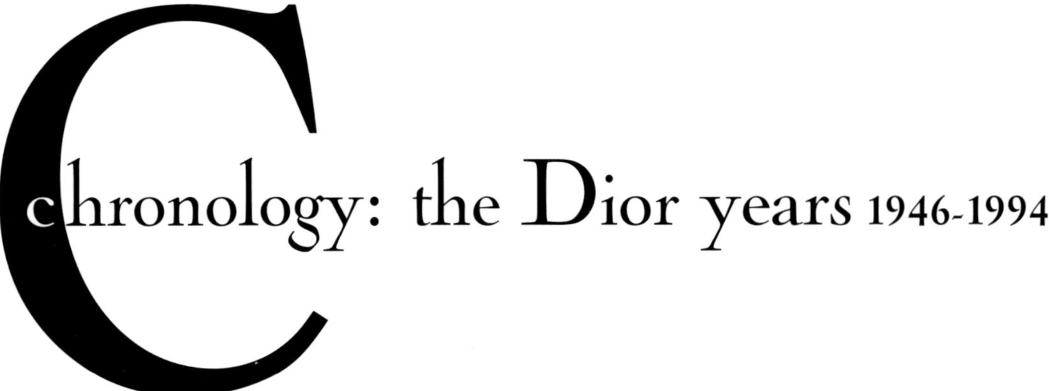

Chronology: the Dior years 1946-1994

1946 8 October: the meeting between Christian Dior and Marcel Boussac leads to the founding of the couture house 'Christian Dior'.

1947 12 February: presentation of the first collection, Spring-Summer 1947, with two lines *Corolle* (Corolla) and *En huit* (Figure eight). 'Christian Dior has revolutionized Couture, rather like the Marne Taxis have saved France', proclaims the very influential editor of *Harper's Bazaar*, Carmel Snow. The New Look was born. Christian Dior is awarded the Oscar of Haute Couture by Mr Neiman Marcus in Dallas, Texas. The house has ninety employees, a turnover of 1.3 million francs and accounts for 75 per cent of all French haute couture exports. October: founding of Parfums Christian Dior. Creation of the perfume Miss Dior.

1948 31 July to 13 August: a Christian Dior parade of fifty-five original and adapted garments, organised by the department store David Jones, is held in Australia. 28 October: founding of Christian Dior New York, Inc for luxurious ready-to-wear and accessories. Founding of Christian Dior Perfumes New York, Inc. In Paris, opening of Christian Dior Furs and a millinery department. 1948 Spring-Summer collection: *Zig-Zag* line (airy flights and geometric designs). 1948–49 Autumn-Winter collection: *Cyclone* line (under the sign of wings).

1949 Christian Dior is the first couturier to sign a licence contract. First stocking licence in the United States: Christian Dior Hosiery. Christian Dior invents the pointed reinforced stocking heel. The Kings and Queens Ball given by Comte Etienne de Beaumont: Christian Dior comes dressed as a lion, in a costume made by Pierre Cardin, former *Premier d'Atelier* (head of workroom) at Christian Dior. 1949 Spring-Summer collection: *Trompe-l'Oeil* line (pocket and décolleté effects). 1949–50 Autumn-Winter collection: *Milieu du siècle* (Mid-century) line (airy and loose-fitting cut). Over 1200 dresses are ordered in eight days.

1950 First tie licence in the United States: Christian Dior Ties. Founding in Paris of the Christian Dior Diffusion department, responsible for wholesale, export and licence agreements. Christian Dior is awarded the *Légion d'Honneur* by the Ministry of Trade and Commerce. Dresses made for Marlene Dietrich for Alfred Hitchcock's film *Stage fright*. 1950 Spring-Summer collection: *Verticale* (Vertical) line (neat and flowing). 1950–51 Autumn-Winter collection: *Oblique* (Oblique) line (pink and grey velvet).

1951 Creation of the stocking department. Creation of Dior Sport, ribbed stockings in four colours. The personnel now number 900. The Beistegui Ball at the Labia Palace in Venice, for which Christian Dior designs several costumes and some spectacular capes. With Salvador Dali, he creates a living painting entitled *The giants*. The book *Je suis couturier* by Christian Dior is published by Conquistador. 1951 Spring-Summer collection: *Ovale* (Oval) line (constructed/natural line). 1951–52 Autumn-Winter collection: *Longue* (Long) line (entirely new proportions).

1952 Founding of Christian Dior Models Ltd in London. 1952 Spring-Summer collection: *Sinueuse* (Sinuous) line (blousons and sweaters). 1952–53 Autumn-Winter collection: *Profilée* (Profile) line (shapely waists and curves).

1953 Founding of the Christian Dior Delman Company, manufacturing made-to-measure shoes designed by Roger Vivier. 1953 Spring-Summer collection: *Tulipe* (Tulip) line (fuller bust, slender hips). 1953–54 Autumn-Winter collection: *Vivante* (Alive) line (inspired by the Eiffel Tower and the domes of Paris; nicknamed the Shock Look in England, because the skirts are shortened to 16 inches, about 40 cm, above the ground).

1954 Opening of Christian Dior Ltd in London. The House of Christian Dior Paris employs a thousand people and is located in five buildings, with twenty-eight workrooms. 1954 Spring-Summer collection: *Muguet* (Lily-of-the-valley) line (volume of hat, bust and skirt). 1954–55 Autumn-Winter collection: *H-line* (the Flat Look, nicknamed the String Bean line).

1955 Opening of the boutique at the corner of rue François 1er. Opening of the Gifts–Tableware department. 3 August: a lecture by Christian Dior at the Sorbonne titled 'Aesthetics of fashion' before 4000 students. 'Doesn't fashion unite the two spirits of geometry and fineness?', he said. Yves Saint Laurent, young winner of the wool design contest, for which Christian Dior was a member of the jury in 1953, is engaged to work at the studio. He becomes the only assistant Christian Dior ever had. Christian Dior designs Olivia de Havilland's wedding dress. 1955 Spring-Summer collection: *A-line* (a contrast of waisted shapes with diagonals). 1955 Autumn-Winter collection: *Y-line* (simplicity and length).

1956 Fourteen dresses made for Ava Gardner for the film *The little hut* by Mark Robson. Twenty-five thousand customers pass through the Christian Dior salons in a single season. Publication by Amiot-Dumont of Christian Dior's memoirs *Christian Dior et Moi*. Launch of the perfume Diorissimo. 1956 Spring-Summer collection: *Flèche* (Arrow) line (slenderised and feminine). 1956–57 Autumn-Winter collection: *Aimant* (Magnet) line (rounded shapes).

1957 4 March: Christian Dior appears on the cover of *Time Magazine*. The House of Christian Dior alone accounts for over 55 per cent of French haute couture exports and employs 1300 people. 1957 Spring-Summer collection: *Libre* (Free) line (free waist, volumes and lengths). 1957–58 Autumn-Winter collection: *Fuseau* (Spindle) line (a curvy, stream-lined look). 24 October: Christian Dior is struck down by a heart attack. Yves Saint Laurent takes over as artistic director of the house. November to December: David Jones, in association with the *Australian Women's Weekly*, presents a complete Christian Dior Show in Australia. Eighty-three spectacular original Christian Dior creations are presented by seven Dior mannequins.

1958 Marc Bohan is appointed artistic director of Christian Dior London. Yves Saint Laurent presents his first collection, 1958 Spring-Summer: *Trapèze* (Trapezium) line (inspired by the Florentine era and the Renaissance).

1959 12 to 16 June: first presentation in Moscow of the Christian Dior haute couture collection, designed by Yves Saint Laurent.

1960 Yves Saint Laurent designs Olivia de Havilland's gown for the Academy Awards ceremony. Yves Saint Laurent leaves Christian Dior. He is succeeded by Marc Bohan, who becomes Christian Dior's artistic director and designs the haute couture collections.

1961 Marc Bohan presents his first collection, the 1961 Spring-Summer haute couture collection: *Slim Look* (garden dresses, printed chiffon on taffeta background). Elizabeth Taylor orders twelve gowns.

1964 Marc Bohan designs costumes for the theatre, opera, ballet and cinema. He dresses Juliette Greco for her show at the Olympia Theatre, Annie Girardot for the Arthur Miller play *After the fall* and Marie Bell in *Madame Princesse* by Félicien Marceau.

1965 Mr Manteau, in charge of the haute fourrure collections since 1957, introduces colours into furs and creates the first bronze-tinted green coat.

1966 Launch of the men's eau de toilette Eau Sauvage.

1967 11 September: presentation of the first collection of Christian Dior women's ready-to-wear, Miss Dior, designed by Philippe Guibourgé. Creation of the *Baby Dior* line. Marc Bohan designs the wedding and coronation dress for the Empress Farah Diba and the gowns worn by her ladies-in-waiting. 1967 Spring-Summer haute couture collection: *Safari line*.

1968 Frédéric Castet becomes responsible for Haute Fourrure at Christian Dior Paris. Marc Bohan designs the costumes for the Joseph Losey film *Cérémonies Secrètes*.

1969 Launch of the first Christian Dior make-up range.

1970 Creation of the Christian Dior Monsieur line, directed by Marc Bohan. Marc Bohan designs Brigitte Bardot's costumes for *L'Ours et la Poupée* by Michel Deville. 1970 Spring-Summer haute couture collection: *Maxi line* (Russian-inspired).

1972 Launch of the perfume Diorella.

1973 Creation of the ready-to-wear furs collection by Frédéric Castet. Launch of Hydra-Dior, the first range of skin-care products.

1975 Inspired by the retrospective exhibition at the Grand Palais, Marc Bohan designs his 1975 Spring-Summer haute couture collection: on a *Pointilliste* theme.

1976 Marc Bohan designs the Queen of Sweden's bridal gown.

1977 Celebration of Christian Dior's thirtieth anniversary at the Lido de Paris.

1979 Launch of the perfume Dioressence.

1980 Gérard Penneroux is appointed designer of the Christian Dior Monsieur line.

1981 On the occasion of the marriage of HRH the Prince of Wales and Lady Diana Spencer, 29 July, Marc Bohan designs dresses for Princess Grace of Monaco, Princess Alexandra of Yugoslavia and Mrs Pamela Hicks, Lord Mountbatten's niece.

1983 The *Dé d'Or* is awarded to Marc Bohan for his 1983 Spring-Summer haute couture collection. Dominique Morlotti replaces Gérard Penneroux and is appointed designer of the Christian Dior Monsieur line and director of the men's design studio.

1984 Creation of Christina Onassis's bridal gown. Launch of the eau de toilette Eau Sauvage Extrême. 1984–85 Autumn-Winter haute couture collection: *Klimt et Pollock*.

1985 April: Bernard Arnault, chairman of the Financière Agache Group, main shareholder, is appointed chairman and managing director of the Christian Dior Company. Launch of the perfume Poison, worldwide best-seller. Grand Ball at the castle of Vaux-le-Vicomte.

1986 First presentation of the haute fourrure collection by Frédéric Castet in China.

1987 To celebrate the fortieth anniversary of the House of Christian Dior, a retrospective is held at the Musée des Arts de la Mode, *Hommage à Christian Dior 1947–1957*. An important book titled *Dior* is published by les Editions du Regard.

1988 The couture and perfume activities, divided in 1968 when Parfums Christian Dior was sold to Moët-Hennessy, are brought back together within the same group. Second *Dé d'Or* awarded to Marc Bohan for his 1988–89 Autumn-Winter haute couture collection.

1989 Gianfranco Ferré succeeds Marc Bohan. He is appointed designer of the Christian Dior Haute Couture, Haute Fourrure, Women's Ready-to-Wear and Fur Collections. Gianfranco Ferré also sets all the trends and directives for the Christian Dior women's designs. In July his first haute couture collection, 1989–90 Autumn-Winter, *Ascot-Cecil Beaton*, is honoured by the *Dé d'Or*. 23 October: presentation of the first 1990 Spring-Summer women's ready-to-wear collection designed by Gianfranco Ferré. Opening of the Christian Dior Boutique in Hawaii.

1990 The Group Christian Dior, a holding company resulting from the interests successively acquired from the capital of LVMH, is now the largest luxury group in the world (excluding the car industry), highly positioned economically as well as in terms of brand image. Opening of the New York and Los Angeles Christian Dior boutiques.

1991 4 December: Christian Dior is quoted at the Paris Stock Exchange. The Christian Dior Group reaches a turnover of over 22 billion francs. Couture alone generates a volume of over 6 million francs. Launch of the perfume Dune: a grand ball is given at the castle of Vaux-le-Vicomte.

1992 Patrick Lavoix is appointed artistic director of Christian Dior Monsieur. Relaunch of the perfume Miss Dior. 3 July: presentation of the first 1993 Spring-Summer men's ready-to-wear collection: *Paris tout simplement, Dior naturellement* (Quite simply Paris, naturally Dior).

1993 Launch of the perfume Tendre Poison.

1994 July: an important retrospective, *Christian Dior: the magic of fashion*, is held at the Powerhouse Museum, Sydney, Australia.

Compiled by Marika Genty, Christian Dior

Catalogue of the exhibition

Design Themes
The New Look

BAR
Spring-Summer 1947
Corolle (Corolla) line
Suit; jacket in raw silk shantung with
suit collar and basque. Fine-pleated
skirt in black woollen fabric.
UFAC, Donated by the House of
Christian Dior, 1958 *(pictured)*

ADELAIDE
Spring-Summer 1948
Envol (Flight) line
Evening gown in black tulle trimmed
with bands of peach satin worn with
evening coat in peach-coloured silk,
satin with old-gold braid border and
three-quarter-length cuffed sleeves.
UFAC, Donated by Mrs Brodie

Dior Alphabet
TAMANACO
Autumn-Winter 1954
H-line
Ensemble in black silk faille. Short,
belted jacket, rounded collar in white
velvet draped over shoulders and
caught with two bows in black faille.
Straight skirt.
UFAC, Donated by Mrs Kaindl

ZELIE
Autumn-Winter 1954
H-line
Dress in black silk faille, high collar
with optional shawl effect. Double
buttoning, double breasted. Low
waist, skirt gathered at hips and back.
Dress belonged to Mrs Quinet-
Vournassov, ex-wife of the editor of
Combat magazine.
Christian Dior Archives

A
Spring-Summer 1955
A-line
Suit in wool and steel grey silk,
A-line. Long double-breasted button-
ing jacket, suit collar, flaring at the
hips. Straight-necked, short-sleeved
bodice over a wide-pleated skirt.
Dress worn by Mrs Olivia de
Havilland at her wedding.
Christian Dior Archives *(pictured)*

ALLIANCE
Spring-Summer 1955
A-line
Dress in sky blue linen, short sleeves,
turn-back collar decorated with a
large flower in pale blue silk, front-
fastening with four fabric-covered
buttons, low waist, flat-pleated skirt.
UFAC, Donated by Mrs Kaindl

HISTORIETTE (Short story)
Autumn-Winter 1955
Y-line
Short-sleeved cocktail dress in red
silk faille, V-neckline, flared skirt.
Dress belonged to Hélène Gordon-
Lazareff, founder of *Elle* magazine,
and mother of the donor.
UFAC, Donated by Mrs Michèle
Rosier

VOYAGEUR (Voyager)
Autumn-Winter 1955
Y-line
Suit in grey herringbone wool by
Raimon. Short, belted jacket, double-
breasted buttoning, with grey silk
chemisette. Straight skirt with
double-breasted buttoning like jacket.
Generous, double-buttoning stole.
Christian Dior Archives
Reproduction 1987

Movement
DELPHINE
Autumn-Winter 1956
Aimant (Magnet) line
Cocktail dress in anthracite grey
silk faille. Crossover neckline, full
skirt. Bow effect at waist formed
by a loop and a fringed tie.
Christian Dior Archives

CURAÇAO
Autumn-Winter 1954
H-line
Cocktail dress in ivory silk faille. Low-
necked bustier top with wide, gath-
ered straps. Dropped waist. Wide
skirt with bow effect on left hip.
Christian Dior Archives

TOURBILLON (Whirlwind)
Autumn-Winter 1956
Aimant (Magnet) line
Short dress in pale green mousseline
silk. Spaghetti-strap bodice. Skirt
overlaid with four wave-like flounces
of mousseline.
UFAC, Donated by Mrs Kaindl

ZERLINE
Autumn-Winter 1957
Fuseau (Spindle) line
Afternoon dress in black silk taffeta,
fully overlaid by a large cape collar,
sleeveless, front zip fastening.
UFAC, Donated by Mrs de Bord

1951
Autumn-Winter 1950
Oblique line
Ensemble in spotted, fashioned silk.
Long-sleeved bodice with suit collar,
extended with two intertwined ties
draped at the waist. Straight, front-
buttoning skirt. Overskirt made up of
two gathered tails of different lengths.
UFAC, Donated by Mrs Brès

FAVORI (Favourite)
Autumn-Winter 1950
Oblique line
Suit in grey wool flannel. Belted jack-
et with asymmetrical tie which passes
under the belt on the left-hand side.
Straight skirt, mid-calf length.
Christian Dior Archives
Reproduction 1987

CAPRICE
Spring-Summer 1948
Zig-Zag line
Dress in royal blue wool. Fitted
bodice, V-neckline, long cuffed
sleeves. Zig-Zag line skirt, belted
at the waist.
Dress once belonged to Mrs
Newman.
Christian Dior Archives

COCOTTE (Sweetie)
Autumn-Winter 1948
Envol (Flight) line
Afternoon dress in black and white
hound's-tooth check wool. Straight
cut, front buttoning, suit collar. Calf
length. Skirt gathered up into back in
a double flounce to form a bustle
dropping into a large box pleat.
Black patent leather belt.
Christian Dior Archives
Reproduction 1987 *(pictured)*

PETIT DINER (Cosy dinner)
Autumn-Winter 1948
Ailée (Winged) line
Dress in black silk faille with brown
highlights. Plunging V-neckline front
and back, straight skirt with loop effect
down the sides, wide draped belt.
Dress once belonged to Mrs Newman.
Christian Dior Archives

CHERIE (Dearest)
Spring-Summer 1947
Corolle (Corolla) line
Afternoon dress in navy blue silk
taffeta. Sleeveless fitted bodice.
Pleated skirt, pleats stitched over hips.
Christian Dior Archives
Reproduction 1983

PICARDIE (Picardy)
Spring-Summer 1953
Tulipe (Tulip) line
Two-piece dress in silk printed with
red and pink flowers on a grey background. Short-sleeved bodice, round
neck, four fabric-covered buttons in
front. Wide skirt with pleated gussets.
UFAC, Donated by Mrs Kaindl

Embroidery

TROPIQUES (Tropics)
Autumn-Winter 1948
Ailée (Winged) line
Black broadcloth jacket with basques,
embroidered with gilt beads, sequins
and peacock feathers in a leaf and
flower pattern, high neck, long
sleeves with musketeer cuffs.
UFAC, Donated by Mrs Brodie

NEGUS
Autumn-Winter 1948
Ailée (Winged) line
Long-sleeved bolero in green silk vel-
vet embroidered on the upper half
and back in gold thread, dotted with
coloured beads and teardrop pearls.
Christian Dior Archives

LAHORE
Autumn-Winter 1948
Ailée (Winged) line
Midnight blue silk bolero, emphasising
the shoulders, embroidered in silver
thread and pearls around the neckline.
Ties in a bow at base of neckline.
Of the ensemble, only the bolero
features in the exhibition.
Dress worn by the Duchess of
Windsor.
Christian Dior Archives

SOIREE DE BAGDAD

(Baghdad evening)
Autumn-Winter 1955
Y-line
Short evening dress in ivory silk satin,
embroidered with blue and translucent
palmettes, gold and silver thread, pearls
and diamantes. Three-quarter sleeves,
square neckline. Skirt flares out in two
scissor panels back and front.
UFAC, Donated by Mr and Mrs
Weinberg

BYZANCE (Byzantium)

Autumn-Winter 1957
Fuseau (Spindle) line
Evening ensemble: gown in red silk
lamé brocade, embroidered with
sequins, gold thread and coloured
stones in a medallion motif. Straight
dress, crew neck, sleeveless.
Dress once belonged to Mrs Herrera
de Ulstar.
Christian Dior Archives

VILMORIN

Spring-Summer 1952
Sinueuse (Sinuous) line
Afternoon dress in white organza
embroidered with daisies. Short-
sleeved bodice with round neckline
and small bertha-style collar.
UFAC, Donated by Mrs Arturo Lopez-
Willshaw

MAY

Spring-Summer 1953
Tulipe (Tulip) line
Evening gown in white organza,
embroidered with green leaves and
pink flowers, strapless cupped bustier
trimmed with an organza scarf draped
over the shoulders. Very wide skirt
over a stiff tulle petticoat.
Worn by Mrs Lazard, mother
of the donor.
UFAC, Donated by Mrs de Bord
(pictured)

MUGUET (Lily-of-the-valley)

Spring-Summer 1957
Libre (Free) line
Cocktail dress in white silk organdie
embroidered around the square neck
and on the skirt with lilies-of-the-
valley by Barbier. Full skirt. Matching
coat, without embroidery.
Dress worn by Mrs Alec Weisweiller.
Christian Dior Archives

MINUIT (Midnight)

Autumn-Winter 1948
Ailée (Winged) line
Black silk velvet decorated with black silk
flowers and tassels. High collar, long,
cuffed sleeves. Pétillault velvet from Lyon.
UFAC, Donated by Mrs Brodie

EVENING COAT

Autumn-Winter 1949
Evening coat in black silk faille and
velvet, embroidered with jet and
woollen felt. Frock coat style.
Embroidered velvet ties form the
collar. Long sleeves. Embroidered
velvet panels on coat skirt.
Christian Dior Archives

LACE EVENING DRESS

1953
Evening dress in guipure lace
decorated with diamante flowers,
cupped strapless bodice.
Once belonged to Mrs Vincent Auriol,
wife of the President of the Republic of
France.
UFAC, Donated by Mr Paul Auriol

Dior Wardrobe
The Suits

AVENTURE (Adventure)

Spring-Summer 1948
Envol (Flight) line
Suit. Short, woollen jacket in black and
white hound's-tooth check, flared back.
Mid-length straight skirt, front buttoning.
Christian Dior Archives
Reproduction 1987 *(pictured)*

TOUR DU MONDE

(Around the world)
Spring-Summer 1954
Muguet (Lily-of-the-valley) line
Suit in grey Dormeuil flannel with white
thread. Blouson jacket with shawl collar
and long sleeves.
V-necked bodice with fine straps.
Full skirt with wide, flat pleats.
Christian Dior Archives
Donated by Countess Renée
de Chambrun

ANGLOMANIE (Anglomania)
Spring-Summer 1955
A-line
Dormeuil woollen fabric in black and white Prince of Wales check. Sleeveless dress with pleated skirt. Short jacket with suit collar.
UFAC, Donated by Mrs Kaindl

NORMANDIE (Normandy)
Spring-Summer 1957
Libre (Free) line
Ensemble in grey woollen fabric. Straight-cut, short-sleeved jacket. Straight skirt with side splits. Stole in the same material, with pocket.
UFAC, Donated by Mrs Lucie Noel

GIRELLE (Girella)
Autumn-Winter 1953
Vivante (Lively) line
Ensemble in light blue wool tweed. Backless dress. Belted long-sleeved jacket, collarless, three buttons and two pockets.
UFAC, Donated by Mrs Kaindl

UNESCO
Autumn-Winter 1949
Milieu du siècle (Mid-century) line
Belted, double-breasted jacket in black wool serge. Draped collar trimmed with a second collar in black velvet. Straight skirt.
UFAC, Donated by Mrs Kaindl

CACHOTIER (Gaoler)
Spring-Summer 1951
Ovale line
Short jacket in ivory silk shantung, fastening below the bust with two buttons. Plunging, oval-shaped neckline. Three-quarter sleeves. Dress in steel-grey alpaca, straight skirt, square neckline, short sleeves. Black leather belt.
Christian Dior Archives
Reproduction 1987

Day Dresses

LONDRES (London)
Autumn-Winter 1950
Oblique line
Dress in black woollen fabric. Bodice with turnover collar. Small triangular opening below collar, trimmed with four buttons each side. Long sleeves. Straight skirt, fastened like 'deck-hand's trousers' with two rows of four buttons.
UFAC, Donated by Mrs Brès

BONNE FORTUNE (Good fortune)
Spring-Summer 1950
Verticale (Vertical) line
Afternoon dress in grey wool pepper and salt weave. Fitted bodice with Danton collar. Shirt-front effect with vertical welted pockets on the bust, and three buttons. Wide skirt with trompe-l'oeil stitched pleat effect. Curved belt in black patent leather. Dress once belonged to Mrs Newman.
Christian Dior Archives

NEW YORK
Autumn-Winter 1953
Coat-dress in black wool cashmere. Draped V-neckline. Belted. Wide front button panel with five mother-of-pearl buttons. Long, cuffed sleeves. This design was created for the 'Christian Dior New York' collection.
Christian Dior Archives

MYOSOTIS (Forget-me-not)
Spring-Summer 1949
Trompe l'oeil line
Forget-me-not-blue wool and silk frock coat. Scooped neckline, two metallic buttons. Three-quarter-length cuffed sleeves.
Christian Dior Archives
Donated by Mrs Leppert

Afternoon Dresses

TOURBILLON (Whirlwind)
Autumn-Winter 1957
Fuseau (Spindle) line
Black wool crêpe dress. Tank-top neckline. Skirt with fluted pleats. Front-tying belt. Bolero with tiny short sleeves.
Christian Dior Archives
Donated by Nicole Jury

PROMESSE (Promise)
Autumn-Winter 1957
Fuseau (Spindle) line
Dress in black woollen fabric. Sleeveless, wide collar also in black wool. Bell-shaped skirt, front zip fastening.
UFAC, Donated by Mrs Malitte Matta

DIORAMA
Autumn-Winter 1947
Corolle (Corolla) line
Dress in black wool crêpe. Fitted, short-sleeved bodice. Waist cinched with black leather belt. Very full skirt finished with black braid, like the collar. This dress required 26.70 x 1.3 metres of fabric, plus 42.50 metres of black braid. It took 230 hours to complete and weighs over 3 kilograms.
Christian Dior Archives
Reproduction 1987

PAPILLON (Butterfly)
Spring-Summer 1948
Envol (Flight) line
Afternoon dress in petrol-blue silk taffeta with white spots. Fitted, front-buttoning bodice with a large, draped collar, worn over a bustier with straps. Wide skirt with box-pleat effect on the sides.
Once belonged to Mrs Newman.
Christian Dior Archives

ABANDON

Autumn-Winter 1948
Ailée (Winged) line
Dress in black woollen fabric. Draped
neck on asymmetrical, low-cut fitted
bodice. Three-quarter-length cuffed
sleeves. Full, calf-length skirt.
Christian Dior Archives
Reproduction 1987 *(pictured)*

JEAN-PIERRE GRÉDY

Spring-Summer 1952
Sinueuse (Sinuous) line
Cocktail ensemble in black Starella
silk taffeta. Short-sleeved camisole
top, overlaid at the front and tied.
Very wide skirt, gathered at the waist
then nipped in at knee length.
Overblouse in fuchsia pink mousseline. Draped oval neckline, fastened
with three buttons.
Christian Dior Archives

Cocktail Dresses

ATOUT COEUR (Hearts are trumps)
Spring-Summer 1955
A-line
Raspberry red silk faille dress. Wide
cradle-cut neckline, off the shoulders
and caught at the back on the left
hand side with a long fringed bow and
tie. Close-fitting bodice, dropped
waist. Wide box-pleated skirt.
Christian Dior Archives

BAL DE PRINTEMPS (Spring ball)
Spring-Summer 1956
Ensemble in straw yellow wool-silk mix
by Staron. Short, collarless evening coat,
trapeze cut, embroidered with multi-
coloured flowers in silk thread and sequins
by Rébé. Cradle-cut bustier top,
decorated with three little bows on the
straps and in the centre of the neckline.
Dropped waist, wide skirt.
This design was created especially for
HRH Princess Grace of Monaco. It is a
short version of 'Bal de Printemps'
(Spring ball). The dress also appeared in
the Autumn-Winter collection for 1956
under the name 'Colinette'.
Christian Dior Archives

BOSPHORE (Bosphorus)
Autumn-Winter 1956
Aimant (Magnet) line
Dress in midnight blue silk velvet
embroidered by Rébé with pearls,
gold thread and emerald green cabo-
chons. Low-cut, strapped bustier.
Princess cut. Short jacket with wide
sleeves, no embroidery.
Christian Dior Archives

VENEZUELA
Autumn-Winter 1957
Fuseau (Spindle) line
Salmon pink silk faille. Low V-cut
bodice, crossover, buttoned at back,
sleeveless. Full skirt.
Worn by Mrs Bernard Dhéran,
daughter of the donor.
UFAC, Donated by Countess de
Latour de Geay *(pictured)*

Evening Dresses

PERUVIENNE (Peruvian)
Autumn-Winter 1949
Milieu du siècle (Mid-century) line
Black silk taffeta evening dress cov-
ered in black taffeta leaves, half-cup
bustier top in black velvet. Wide skirt
with taffeta fluting forming a train.
UFAC, Donated by Mrs de Bord

VENEZUELA
Autumn-Winter 1951
Longue (Long) line
Evening gown in red silk organza,
half-cup bustier bodice decorated
with a red faille bow with long ties.
Wide skirt with train.
UFAC, Donated by Mrs Arturo
Lopez-Willshaw

COUP DE THEATRE
Spring-Summer 1951
Ovale (Oval) line
Evening dress in white silk. Bodice
covered in Hérel black tulle and
embroidered with bands of gold thread.
Huge white taffeta bow at waist.
UFAC, Donated by Mrs Citroën

SOIREE A TOLEDE (Toledo evening)
Autumn-Winter 1955
Y-line
Long dress in black silk velvet. Square
neckline, long sleeves. Large band of
black grosgrain at hem. Short cape
with wide black velvet hood.
Once belonged to Mrs Alec
Weisweiller.
Christian Dior Archives

AMADIS
Autumn-Winter 1954
H-line
Ensemble in pale pink silk satin,
embroidered by Rébé with palmettes
in silk thread in various shades of pink
and dotted with tiny diamantes. Long,
close-fitting short-sleeved jacket with
oval, draped collar. Fully embroidered.
Touch of pink satin at the cuffs and
jacket hem. Sheath dress, embroidered
to just below the hips.
Worn by mannequin Victoire in a
parade at Blenheim Palace in 1954 for
HRH Princess Margaret, and the
Duke and Duchess of Marlborough.
Christian Dior Archives

FESTIVAL
Autumn-Winter 1956
Aimant (Magnet) line
Sleeveless dress in white Perceval silk satin
embroidered by Rébé in mother-of-pearl
and white diamantes. Small box pleats
caught in at the back by three bows.
Dress worn by Mrs Arturo Lopez-
Willshaw to an evening party hosted
by Carlos de Beistegui at the Château
de Groussay.
UFAC, Donated by Mrs Semenoff

MUSIQUE DE FETE (Festive music)
Spring-Summer 1955
A-line
Long gown in pale blue silk organza.
High, crossover camisole top with
draped shawl and long sleeves. Very
wide, floating skirt. Belt in the same
fabric decorated with a rose.
Dress belonged to Mrs Alec
Weisweiller.
Christian Dior Archives

Gala Dresses
MEXIQUE (Mexico)
Autumn-Winter 1951
Longue (Long) line
Dress in brown tulle embroidered
with crescent moons in gold thread.
Bustier bodice highlighted by a bow in
brown velvet. Full skirt.
UFAC, Donated by Mrs de Ayala

JUNON (Juno)
Autumn-Winter 1949
Milieu du siècle (Mid-century) line
Gala dress in tulle decorated with
sequins by Dognin in iris blues, re-
embroidered by Rébé in dark blue
and bronze sequins, embroidered
bustier top. Voluminous skirt consist-
ing of petals in tulle and horsehair
flouncing out to the hem and
covered with sequins.
Dress once belonged to Mrs Newman.
Christian Dior Archives *(pictured)*

Bridal Dress
FIDELITE (Fidelity)
Autumn-Winter 1949
Milieu du siècle (Mid-century) line
Silk bridal gown. Extremely close-
fitting bodice in white satin, tiny
shawl collar and long, cuffed sleeves.
Wide skirt in tulle decorated with two
satin ties knotted in a bow at the back,
one-third of the way down the skirt.
Christian Dior Archives
Reproduction 1987

After M. Dior
ETRUSQUE (Etruscan)
Created by Yves Saint Laurent
Spring-Summer 1960
Evening dress in silk taffeta printed
with stylised red poppies on a black
background. Fitting bodice, straight
neck, short sleeves. Short sheath
skirt. Bubble overskirt, short in front,
dipping at the back.

Dress worn by Mrs Olivia de
Havilland for the presentation of the
Academy Awards in 1960.
Christian Dior Archives

GRAND BONHEUR (Great happiness)
Created by Marc Bohan
Autumn-Winter 1961
Evening ensemble: long gown in silver
and white silk satin brocade,
embroidered with diamantes. Fitted
bodice, round collar, sleeveless. Wide
skirt, heavy fall. Very short, fully
embroidered bolero with long sleeves.
Christian Dior Archives

Spirit of Dior
SCALA
Created by Gianfranco Ferré
Autumn-Winter 1989
Silk ball gown. Bustier top embroidered
with flowers and diamantes. Stole in
black organza draped across the shoulders and extended into two long ties
lying down the back. Skirt in raw lace
worn over black tulle petticoats.
Christian Dior Archives

AMOUREUSE (In love)
Created by Gianfranco Ferré
Autumn-Winter 1990
Short cocktail dress. Backless bustier
top in grenadine red silk taffeta.
Draped neckline with V-pleats
crossed over to form two huge bows
above the skirt. Straight skirt in
crushed velvet. Bolero in woven red
and pink wool fabric, embroidered in
tapestry stitch with gold floral motifs.
Christian Dior Archives

ALCOVE
Created by Gianfranco Ferré
Autumn-Winter 1993–94
Bodice bordered by mohair and gold
and red threads; long skirt in flower
print organza; shawl in mohair, silk
and gold and red lamé woven in
traditional weave.
Christian Dior Archives

Further Reading

Ballard, Bettina. *In my fashion*,
Secker & Warburg, London, 1960.

Dior, Christian. *Talking about fashion*,
Hutchinson, London, 1954.

Dior, Christian. *Dior by Dior: the
autobiography of Christian Dior*,
Penguin, Harmondsworth, 1958.

Dorner, Jane. *Fashion in the forties and fifties*,
Ian Allan Ltd, London, 1975.

Giroud, Françoise. *Dior: Christian Dior
1905–1957*, Thames and Hudson,
London, 1987.

Joel, Alexandra. *Best dressed: 200 years of
fashion in Australia*, Collins, Sydney, 1984.

Keenan, Brigid. *Dior in Vogue*, Octopus
Books, London, 1981.

Lynam, Ruth (ed). *Couture*, Doubleday &
Company, New York, 1972.

Musée des Arts de la Mode. *Hommage à
Christian Dior 1947–1957*, Union des Arts
Decoratifs, Paris, 1986.

Photo Credits